The Life and Work of...

Diego Rivera

Adam Schaefer

Heinemann Library
Chicago, Illinois

Design by Heinemann Library
Page layout by Jennifer Lee
Photo research by Alan Gottlieb
Printed and bound in the United States by Lake Book Manufacturing, Inc.

07 06 05
10 9 8 7 6 5 4 3 2

Library of Congress Cataloging-in-Publication Data
Schaefer, A. R. (Adam Richard), 1976-
    Diego Rivera / Adam Schaefer.
      p. cm. -- (The life and work of--)
    Includes bibliographical references and index.
    Summary: Briefly examines the life and work of the twentieth-century
Mexican painter, describing and giving examples of his art.
    Includes bibliographical references and index.
      ISBN 1-40340-288-4 -- ISBN 1-40340-494-1 (pbk.)
      1. Rivera, Diego, 1886-1957--Juvenile literature. 2.
Painters--Mexico--Biography--Juvenile literature. 3. Mural painting and
decoration--Mexico--Juvenile literature. [1. Rivera, Diego, 1886-1957.
2. Artists. 3. Art appreciation.] I. Title. II. Series.
ND259.R5 S33 2003
759.972--dc21   2002004023
[B]   CIP

Acknowledgments
The publisher would like to thank the following for permission to reproduce photographs:

pp. 4, 14, 22, 27 Bettmann/Corbis; pp. 5, 12, 19, 20, 21, 23, 29 Schalkwijk/Art Resource; pp. 6, 8 Danny Lehman/Corbis; pp. 7, 11 Diego Rivera Museum, Guanajuato; p. 9 W. Cody/Corbis; p. 10 Museo de Franz Mayer; pp. 13, 14 Hulton Archive/Getty Images; p. 15 Notre Dame de Paris in the Rain, 1909, Diego Rivera, Mexico City, Museo Nacional de Arte (INBA), Photograph ©1986 The Detroit Institute of Arts; p. 16 Diego Rivera Photographic files/CENIDIAP/INBA; p. 17 The Arkansas Arts Center Foundation Collection: Gift of Abby Rockefeller Mauze, New York, 1955; p. 18 SCALA/Art Resource; p. 24 Detroit Industry: East Wall, 1932-33, Diego M. Rivera, Gift of Edsel B. Ford, photograph © 1932 The Detroit Institute of Arts; p. 25 Detroit Industry: North Wall, 1932-33, Diego M. Rivera, Gift of Edsel B. Ford, photograph © 2001 The Detroit Institute of Arts; p. 26 Diego Rivera Mural Project/City College of San Francisco; p. 28 Diego Rivera Photographic files, CENIDIAP/INBA

Special thanks to Katie Miller for her comments in the preparation of this book.

Some words in this book are in bold, **like this.** You can find out what they mean by looking in the Glossary.

Contents

Who Was Diego Rivera?

Diego Rivera was a Mexican artist. He was a painter. He is famous for painting large, colorful **murals**.

Land and Freedom, 1923–1924

Diego painted what he saw in everyday life. His art was about real people. He liked to paint farmers and other workers.

Early Years

Diego Rivera was born December 8, 1886, in Guanajuato, Mexico. Guanajuato is a large town in Mexico. Diego's mother and father were teachers there.

Diego was very sick as a boy. His father put chalkboards on the walls of Diego's room. Diego drew **murals** on them. In this photograph, Diego is standing outside the house where he grew up.

Going To School

Diego's parents sent him to **military school** when he was 13 years old. Diego hated it. He left and started art school at the San Carlos Academy of Fine Arts. This is a picture of the San Carlos Academy.

Diego was the youngest student at San Carlos. His teachers liked his drawings and **sketches.** One time he won second place in a drawing contest. His prize was a set of oil paints.

9

Big Changes

Diego liked painting more than drawing. He won money for his paintings when he was 18 years old. The next year he had his first **exhibition**. He exhibited this painting.

La Castaneda, 1904

La Era, 1904

Diego painted what he saw in everyday life. He liked to go outside and paint things around him. He especially liked to paint people. He painted people working.

Leaving Mexico

When Diego was 20 years old, he left Mexico and went to Spain. He painted this **self-portrait** while he lived in Spain.

Self-Portrait, 1907

Diego lived in Madrid, the capital city of
Spain. He visited the art museum there.
He studied with a famous Spanish artist
named Eduardo Chicharro.

Visiting Paris

Diego traveled to Paris, France in 1909. Artists from all over the world were living in Paris. Diego learned a lot by talking to other artists and watching them paint.

14

Notre Dame de Paris in the Rain, 1909

While he was in Paris, Diego continued to
paint. He studied with many famous painters.
He started to make a name for himself.
Some art galleries in Europe showed his works.

A New Style

This is a photograph of Diego when he lived in Paris. Artists in Paris wanted to show things from all different angles in one painting. Diego became interested in this idea.

Portrait of Two Women, 1914

Diego started painting in a new style. The style is called **Cubism**. Diego's Cubist paintings show objects from many angles. To do this, Diego used simple shapes.

17

Important Trip

Michelangelo, *Sistine Chapel fresco*, 1510–1512

Diego was learning a lot in Paris, but he wanted to learn more. In 1920, he traveled to Italy to study **Renaissance** art. While he was in Italy he saw many **frescoes**.

18

Creation, 1922–1923

Frescoes are large paintings on walls or ceilings. The frescoes that Diego saw were painted in the 1400s and 1500s. Diego went home to Mexico in 1921. He painted this fresco, based on the art he saw in Italy.

Return to Mexico

When Diego got back to Mexico he married Lupe Marin. He took a job with the government. His job was to help artists find work. He also painted **murals** in government buildings.

Tehuanuas, 1923

Indian Boy and Indian Woman with Corn Stalks, 1926–1927

Diego used what he learned in Italy in his paintings. He painted this mural at a church in Mexico City. Murals like the ones Diego was painting had never been seen before in Mexico.

Taking a New Job

Lupe thought that Diego spent too much time painting. She and Diego were divorced.
In 1929, Deigo married Frida Kahlo. Frida was a painter, too.

The Aztec World, 1929

Also in 1929, Diego became the **director** of the San Carlos Academy of Fine Arts. During this time, he started work on one of his most famous **murals.** The mural was at the Palacio Nacional. It showed the history of Mexico.

Public Art

In the 1930s, Diego started working in the United States. He painted **murals** in Detroit, San Francisco, and New York City. Famous people came to watch Diego paint.

24

Production of Engine and Transmission of Ford V-8, 1932–1933

Diego's murals were almost always in public places. They were on government buildings or at large company offices. Many people could enjoy his art. Art that is put in a place where many people can see it is called **public art.**

Helping a Cause

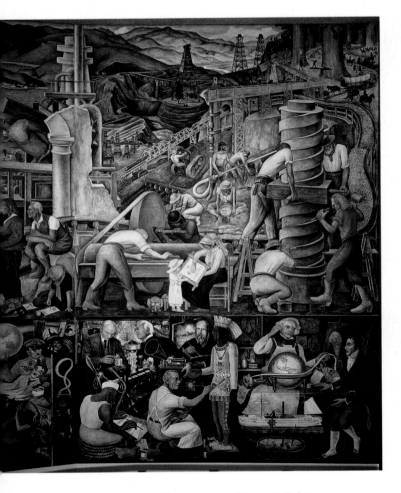

Pan-American Unity, 1940

Diego painted **murals** in many countries. This mural is in a college in San Francisco. Diego wanted to show that people in North America and South America should all work together.

As he got older, Diego painted murals that
showed his political beliefs. His paintings made
some people upset. They did not want politics
mixed with art.

Working Until the End

Diego worked until the final months of his life. He died on November 24, 1957, in his studio in Mexico City. He was 70 years old.

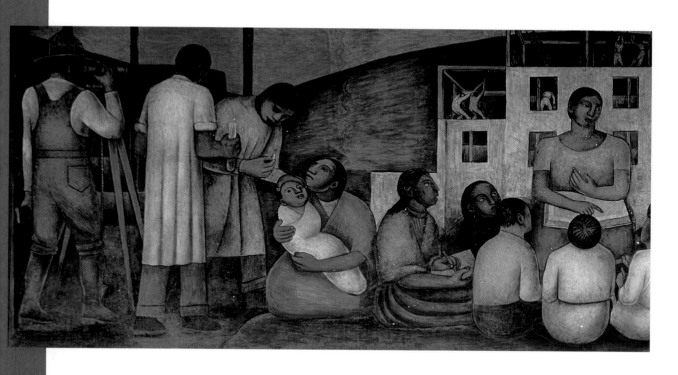

Allegory of California, 1928

People are still amazed by the amount of work that Diego completed in his lifetime. His **murals** can be seen all over the world.

Timeline

1886	Diego Rivera is born, December 8.
1892	The Rivera family moves to Mexico City.
1898	The Spanish American War takes place.
1900	Diego goes to **military school** for two weeks.
	Diego starts classes at San Carlos Academy of Fine Arts.
1906	Diego goes to Spain to study art in Europe.
1909	Diego goes to Paris, France.
1914	World War I begins.
1918	World War I ends.
1920	Diego travels to Italy to study **Renaissance frescoes.**
	Diego returns to Mexico and starts painting large **murals.**
1929	Diego marries Frida Kahlo.
1933	Diego finishes murals at the Detroit Institute of Art.
1935	Diego completes a mural at the Palacio Nacional.
1957	Diego Rivera dies, November 24.

Glossary

Cubism style of art popular in the early 1900s that showed people and things broken down into circles, squares, and triangles instead of showing people and things in a lifelike way. A painting that is made using Cubism is called cubist.

director person who is in charge of a school, office, or project and makes certain everything goes smoothly

exhibition show of works of art in public

fresco painting done on wet plaster so the color soaks in

military school place where people learn to be soldiers

mural picture painted directly onto a wall

political describing a certain belief about how a country should be run

public art paintings or statues that are placed where many people can see them, like city squares, libraries, schools, or large office buildings

Renaissance time from the 1300s to the 1600s in Europe, when there was great new interest in art and learning

self-portrait picture that an artist makes of himself or herself

sketch to draw something quickly without filling in all the details, or a drawing that was made quickly without much detail

Index

More Books to Read

Holland, Gigi. *Diego Rivera*. New York: Raintree Steck-Vaughn Publishers, 1997.

Venezia, Mike. *Diego Rivera*. Danbury, Conn: Children's Press, 1995. An older reader can help you with this book.

More Artwork to See

Niña Parada. 1957. Arizona State University Art Museum. Tempe, Arizona

Sueño. 1932. San Diego Museum. San Diego, California

Mandragora. 1939. San Diego Museum. San Diego, California

Mother and Child. 1927. Worchester Art Museum. Worchester, Massachusetts

Untitled (Head in Profile). 1940. University of Maine Museum of Art. Orono, Maine